**BODYBUILD[ING]
COOKBOO[K]**

RIPPED RECIPES

nutrition in the kitchen for gains in the gym

Build muscle. Burn Fat. Get Shredded....
Chef in the kitchen. Calorie counted recipes with
macronutrient breakdowns to help you get ripped
whether you're bulking, cutting or maintaining.

BODYBUILDING COOKBOOK RIPPED RECIPES

Build Muscle. Burn Fat. Get Shredded.... Chef in the kitchen. Calorie counted recipes with macronutrient breakdowns to help you get ripped whether you're bulking, cutting or maintaining

ISBN: 978-1-913005-08-5

Cover image: under license from shutterstock

DISCLAIMER

CONTENTS

HIGHER CARB RECIPES

SMOOTHIES, SNACKS & TREATS 83

INTRODUCTION

Ripped recipes will start you on a journey towards creating the right building blocks by matching your nutritional needs to your goals.

So you've purchased this book because you want to build muscle. That's great – you've made a decision to change your body, get healthy, lean and feel great. This book will give you an introduction to just how you can help build the body you want through meals and nutrition.

Great bodies are not made in the gym alone. Sure, exercise, activity and workouts are needed and you'll need to work hard but you won't make any of the gains you need unless you start in the kitchen and grasp the building blocks of healthy nutrition which will lead to gains in the gym.

You may already have come to learn that no matter how hard you work in the gym – whether that's hours of cardio or heavy weights, if you don't match that effort in the kitchen you simply won't see the results you want. Put simply: your body cannot develop unless you feed it correctly. It needs to repair itself from the damage and distress caused by lifting weights, it won't burn fat without a deficit in calories but if you don't eat enough you will find that rather than burning fat efficiently your body instead uses precious muscle as energy reserves.
If your goal is 'bulking' (gaining size) you'll find the wrong nutritional choices can result in excess fat gain: demonstrating the potential problems and why many people opt for quick fix diets to try to get the desired results.

It doesn't matter if you think you're not the best cook in the world. This book will teach you how to make great tasting, easy, speedy meals that will compliment all the hard work you do in the gym and help you build muscle, get lean and achieve the body you're happy with.

How? By teaching you the basics in nutritional meals that will match the gains you want to make in the gym.

If you're new to bodybuilding you will likely have heard tales of the bland and boring daily intake of brown rice, oats, broccoli, chicken and eggs that all men and women who are serious about making gains must ingest in order to achieve their goals. Sure, all these ingredients and countless others can make up the perfect diet to complement your workouts and see great results, but for most it's unsustainable long term. If food doesn't taste great, what's the point?

There is a way of cooking meals that taste amazing and still hit your nutritional targets and without being a slave to calorie counting. This collection of ripped recipes will start you on a journey towards creating the right building blocks by matching your nutritional needs to your goals.

UNDERSTANDING NUTRITION

Calories

We all know about calories; too many and you get fat, too little and you can't grow. But what exactly is a calorie? For the purposes of getting a better understanding of your daily intake and the nutritional breakdown required lets explain.

A calorie is a unit of energy. 1cal is measured by the amount of energy required to raise one gram of water by one degree Celsius.
Our bodies require calories to function. Energy is required and used by all our organs to keep them working, for our cells to grow and to undertake the daily activities we do – moving, working, talking – everything requires some energy.
Some calories are called 'empty calories' which refer to foods that are high in energy but low in nutritional value. Everyone requires a different amount of energy per day and therefore a different number of calories based on their age, sex, height, size and level of activity.

So calories are needed for our bodies to function - but how many? As we've learned this depends on different factors such as age, weight, sex and activity. The generic government guidelines in the UK (based on recommendations of the Committee on Medical Aspects of Food Policy, COMA) for adults to maintain healthy levels of weight, which are:

Women 2000 calories per day
Men 2500 calories per day

But this can't really apply to all because:
a) *everyone is different*
b) *it gives us no nutritional breakdown of these calories.*

You may have used one of the many calorie calculators that are freely available to track your food intake. These are very useful tools and are based on huge amounts of data and nutritional science. The problem is they can be confusing and time consuming to use. Accurately tracking every ingredient of every single meal will of course give you precise measurements of your food intake but over time it is unsustainable and will likely result in you gettting fed up and throwing your good food choices out of the window.

The good news is that you can get a real balance to your mealtimes and look forward to enjoying healthy, tasty food by using a basic nutritional formula to match your goals with your nutritional needs.

Our recipes assume that you are active in exercise at least three times per week. On this basis, and in order to achieve steady muscle growth without adding fat, you should apply the following formula to your daily food intake. This formula is widely used a basis for nutritional needs in bodybuilding forums around the world and is made up of the 3 main food energy sources – protein, carbohydrates and fat.

For maintaining your current physique with slow muscle gains over time without adding excess body fat you should consume the following each day:

Protein	Carbohydrates	Healthy Fat
eat 1 gram of protein per pound of body weight per day	eat 1.5 grams of carbs per pound of body weight per day	eat 1 gram of fats per 4 pounds of body weight per day

For a man weighing 170 pounds (77kg) this works out at approx. 2080 calories per day.

If your goal is to build muscle and size then you should increase your carbohydrate intake by approx. **50 grams per day** and your healthy fats by approx. **30 grams per day**. This will put you in a calorie surplus of approx. 500 calories and a total calorie intake of about 2580 cals.

If fat loss is your goal then go the other way and reduce your daily calorie intake by about 500 calories. This time by consuming less carbs and slightly less protein. Drop your carbs by **90 grams per day** and protein by **10 grams per day**. Fat intake should remain the same to keep you feeling fuller (more on that later).

Using the same example of a 170-pound (77kg) man this is how the macro breakdown of each goal would look:

Muscle Gains	Maintenance	Fat Loss
Protein 270g = 680cals	Protein 170g = 680cals	Protein 160g = 640cals
Carbs 300g = 1220cals	Carbs 255g = 1020cals	Carbs 165g = 660cals
Fat = 73g = 657cals	Fat 43g = 387 cals	Fat 43g = 387cals
Total Calories = 2557	Total Calories = 2087	Total Calories = 1687

Macronutrients

You may have heard people talking about their macros. So what exactly are they?
They refer to the main nutritional needs of the body to survive and function and can be broken down into three distinct groups:

Protein   Carbohydrates   Fat

Micronutrients are vitamins and minerals that are still vital to bodily function but are only required in much smaller quantities.

Protein

Protein plays a vital role in the body. It builds ands repairs muscle and helps cells regenerate as well as assisting in the manufacture of hormones and keeping your immune system healthy.

If you work out then you will require more protein then the average person who doesn't. Each time you lift

weights you are causing muscles to tear under the strain. These tiny micro tears need to be repaired and grow stronger and bigger – that's where protein works its magic.
If you don't eat enough protein – you muscles won't grow.

The best source of protein is from food although it can also be obtained through supplements such as whey protein powder. Whilst it is not necessary to get protein through supplements it can be a helpful additional source when consuming higher than average daily levels.

Recommended sources of protein:

Lean chicken, beef, pork & turkey	Jerky
Fish (tuna, salmon, trout, sardines, mackerel, cod, haddock, halibut)	Peanut butter
Eggs	Nuts (unsalted)
Geek yogurt	Quinoa
Cottage cheese	Brown rice
Dried lentils	

Carbohydrates

Carbs do not make you fat! Eating **too many** carbs can make you fat but then so would eating too much protein or fat. The bad press that has unfairly been attributed to carbs stems from the type of carbs consumed.

There are two types of carbohydrate – 'simple' and 'complex'. These are labelled according to where they fall on something called the glycemic index - which ranks how quickly carbs are converted into glucose when consumed on scale 0 to 100.

Carbs when eaten are broken down into glucose and glycogen. Glucose is used as energy which when released into your bloodstream elevates blood sugar levels. This process in turn triggers the pancreas to produce insulin that enables cells to absorb the glucose and obtain energy. When there are high levels of blood sugar and the body does not produce enough insulin then health problems such as Type 2 Diabetes can occur.

Glycogen is excess glucose that is stored in the liver or muscles and then used by your body for a boost of energy. The liver and muscles however can only store a certain amount of glycogen – any excess will be stored as fat. So you can begin to understand why too many carbs can make you store excess fat.

Simple carbs are those that convert to sugar very quickly and therefore rank highly on the glycemic index. These food should be avoided – they can result in temporary 'sugar highs' and long term can lead to insulin resistance and the onset of Type 2 Diabetes as well as heart disease and obesity.

Complex carbs take much longer to break down into energy in the body and rank lower on GI. A lower release in energy avoids the sugar spikes and keeps you feeling fuller for longer and allows the body to store glucose for energy boosts when needed much more efficiently.

Some good carb examples:	Some 'bad' carb examples:
Barley	White potatoes
Red lentils	White bread
Butter beans	French fries
Baked beans	Cheerios
Bananas	White rice
Brown rice	
Wholemeal bread	
Sweet potatoes	
Wholemeal pasta	

Fibrous carbs

Vegetables are all mainly fibrous carbs. They don't elevate blood sugar levels, are low in calories and high in fibre. Aim to eat fibrous carbs with each meal.

Some great fibrous carb examples:
Spinach
Broccoli
Red peppers
Mushrooms,
Kale
Green beans
Squash
Cauliflower

Although it is a complex subject put simply - carbohydrates are not your enemy. They are required for energy and should be consumed each day both pre-exercise to fuel your workout and post exercise to deplete energy stores. Try looking up the glycemic index to familiarise yourself with different foods and where they fall. Avoid carbs that are above 60 in the table.

Fat

Like carbs, fats have also had a rough time of it, often demonised in the world of dieting in particular. Fats contain 4 times as much energy per gram as protein or carbs – so that means 4 times as many calories per gram.

Fats are essential – they are a source of energy, contain fatty acids used for growth development and cell functions, help maintain healthy skin, help form hormones and transport vitamins through the bloodstream.

There are four main types of fat:

Monounsaturated   Polyunsaturated   Saturated   Trans

Monounsaturated
Avocados, olives, olive oil, rapeseed oil, almonds, cashews, hazelnuts, peanuts, pistachios.
Monounsaturated fats can help maintain healthy cholesterol levels and prevent build up in your arteries that lead to heart health problems.

Polyunsaturated

Oily fish, corn oil, sesame oil, flaxseed, pine nuts, sesame seeds, sunflower seeds, walnuts
Polyunsaturated fats can help maintain healthy cholesterol levels and provide essential fatty acids.

Saturated

Processed meats e.g. sausages, hamburgers, hard cheese, whole milk, butter, cream.
Saturated fats can increase the level of cholesterol in your blood. Where possible these fats should be replaced with monounsaturated and polyunsaturated fats.

Trans

Fried foods, takeaways, biscuits, cakes, pastries, margarine.
Trans fats are modified saturated fats generally found in processed foods that have no nutritional value and can increase cholesterol levels significantly. Avoid all trans fats as much as you possibly can.

HOW TO PLAN YOUR MEALS ACCORDING TO YOUR GOALS

Everyone's macro nutritional goals are different. To tailor a unique individual meal plan that suited every person would be impossible in the confines of one book. You could be a man or a woman of any age, you may have an active job or a sedentary one, you might be looking to retain muscle and lose fat or you may wish to gain muscle and size. So you can see therefore that nutritional guidelines and calorie intake will vary hugely according to these goals.

Before you throw down this book in desperation or rush out to pay for one of the ma y on offer just remember the formula that we introduced you to earlier in this chapter. It's all you need to help you get the body you want together with your efforts in the gym.

But how you may ask if my current statistics and goals are different to the next person? The answer is by simply adjusting your protein, carb and fat intake according to your needs. It's really easy to do – all you need is a calculator (don't just rely on mental arithmetic) to hand.

For example, using our earlier formula for a 170-pound man (77kg), if your goal is to **gain muscle** then you should aim to meet the following per day:

Protein	Carbohydrates	Healthy Fat
eat 1 gram of protein per pound of body weight per day	eat 1.8 grams of carbs per pound of body weight per day	eat 1.7 gram of fats per 4 pounds of body weight per day
i.e. 1g x 170 = 170g protein	i.e. 1.8g x 170 = 306g carbs	i.e. 1.7g x 170 ÷ 4 = 72.25g fat

Remember, this is approx. 50g more carbohydrates and 30g more fat per day than the maintenance formula.

So all you need to do to accurately measure your nutrition and make sure you are hitting the correct macros is select recipes that you like the look of then add up the total protein, carbs and fat for all recipes to give you a total daily macronutritional tally. If you plan to eat 3 meals in a day it is unlikely that you will find 3 meals that will exactly hit your targets, but don't worry you can use the snack section to bump op your intake where you need to.

As time moves on and you become more confident in your cooking and understanding of your macro nutritional needs and calorie intake you may wish to adjust our recipes to tailor them more to your own requirements. For example you may wish to increase the portion of protein in any given meals or perhaps reduce the carbs.

This is easily done and just requires a fuller understanding of the macro content of each food. For example 100g of skinless chicken breast contains 24g protein and 158 calories. You may wish to increase the protein in a particular recipe to 40g in which case this would require 170g of chicken breast. What you need to be aware of when managing your food intake is that this particular increase would result in an additional 11.4g of fat and 111 calories.

While you can easily adjust the ingredients of our ripped recipes to suit your own needs – just remember that if you are increasing/decreasing protein/carbs/fat you may also need to make slight adjustments in the other ingredients up or down to get the consistency of the recipe right.

So this method is certainly possible and as we mentioned earlier there are a number of apps which help to track calories however this is certainly a time consuming process so to start with we recommend using our recipes and picking them according to their macro content to hit your goals.

To make navigating the recipes in the book easier we have divided it into two main sections:

Within each section is a selection of delicious, lean, simple breakfast, lunch, dinner and snack recipes. You may select recipes from both sections as long as the tally at the end of the day matches your macro needs according to the formula.

To further understand how calories are calculated based on your macros you should know that protein, carbs and fats all have their own measurement of energy and therefore calories.

Protein	Carbohydrates	Fats
1g = 4 calories	1g = 4 calories	1g = 9 calories

So you can see that fats have more than twice as many calories and are more energy rich that both protein and carbs put together.

If we again go back to our example of a 170-pound (77kg) man who wishes to gain muscle we can easily calculate the calories needed based on the formula:

Protein	Carbohydrates	Healthy Fat
eat 1 gram of protein per pound of body weight per day	eat 1.8 grams of carbs per pound of body weight per day	eat 1.7 gram of fats per 4 pounds of body weight per day
i.e. 1g x 170 = 170g protein	i.e. 1.8g x 170 = 306g carbs	i.e. 1.7g x 170 ÷ 4 = 72.25g fat
170g protein = 680 calories	**306g carbs = 1224 calories**	**72.25g fats = 650.25 calories**

Therefore total daily calorie intake using this formula = approx. 2554

The key with planning, adjusting and prepping your meals is not to get too weighed (pardon the pun) down with detail. Sure it's important to try to get your weights and measurements accurate, but don't obsess over it. Give yourself a month of following these guidelines and you will be surprised how it starts to become second nature. You will start to recognise what 200g of chicken looks like (always weigh it on the scales though) or how many carbs are in a portion of rice. Your shopping habits will begin to change and you'll find yourself automatically looking for lean meats and fresh greens instead of the frozen junk isle. Our recipes will begin to introduce you to a lean, healthy and muscle building approach to your meals without sacrificing on taste.

Prepping your meals

The key to making sure you hit your macros every time is planning and prepping each one in advance. There is no use in waiting until lunchtime to think about what you are going to have to eat. By that time you will be hungry and are likely to want to eat quickly without having to think about what your meal is – this is where poor choices are made so try to plan ahead.

If you're a pro you could plan a whole week of meals, making sure you have all the ingredients to hand to prepare and make ahead your meals for the week. If you can't do that then spend 10 mins browsing through our recipes the night before making a note of what you plan to make for all your meals the following day and making sure you have all the ingredients.

The only way that you will see changes in your body is if you match the time you spending working out with time in the kitchen so it's really important that you make the effort and think ahead about your meals.

Frequency

How often you eat is a matter of personal choice. Most prefer breakfast, lunch and dinner with perhaps a snack between meals. This is absolutely fine if that's what works for you. If you find however that you are hungry between meals you can split your meals so that you eat 5-6 meals and eat approx. every 3 hours. This is helpful if you are in a calorie deficit; if you feel hungry, eating smaller meals more often you can keep hunger at bay.

If you are in a calorie surplus and find large meals too much in one sitting, you may find it easier to split your meals into smaller portions but more often.
Adopt whichever way works for you and your lifestyle as long as you hit your macros accurately in a day.

KEY INGREDIENTS

You will notice from our recipes that there are some champion ingredients that we use a lot. That's because they are really good for you, easy to source and cook. It's worth stocking up on some of these key ingredients so you always have them to hand.

Eggs	Sweet potatoes
Coconut oil & olive oil	Blueberries
Coconut milk	Chillies
Avocado	Spinach
Herbs & spices	Broccoli
Feta cheese	Raspeberries

SNACKS

We've included a small selection of snacks and sweet treats. These recipes are great in-between fillers and can satisfy cravings but more importantly help meet your macro targets in a day.

CHEAT MEALS

You may have heard this term. When you are sticking to a particular diet plan (either weight loss or muscle gain) the theory is you can throw caution to the wind and 'reward' yourself with something indulgent every now and again.

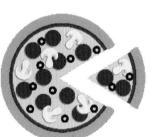

Let's face it, sticking to a nutritional plan takes a lot of effort and there will be many times when you want to 'throw in the towel'. It's for this reason that many reward themselves periodically with a 'cheat' meal.

What exactly a cheat meal is will vary from person to person but a word of warning.... If you decide to give yourself a break by opting for a meal that does not stick to your macro plan, that's OK, but make sure it's just a 'cheat meal' – not a 'cheat' day or a 'cheat' weekend. You can so easily undo all the good work you have done in a week with a blow-out weekend.

If you're planning a 'cheat' meal try to not to go too overboard – for example you could opt to try to stay in the parameters of your daily calorie limit but ignore your nutrition. Try not to overeat or drink too much alcohol– you can still award yourself a beer or two or one of your all time favourite meals – just don't gorge.

Also – don't make cheat meals a regular occurrence. Once every few weeks at most. Keep your eye on your goal.

ALCOHOL

Alcohol is often referred to as having 'empty' calories. This is because it contains nearly as much energy and therefore calories as fat. The energy has little in the way of nutrients and the body cannot process alcohol in the same was as it can protein, carbs and fat. The body will prioritise breaking down alcohol before fat and carbs so you can see how it can inhibit your fitness goals.

Avoid alcohol when you can. If it's not realistic to completely abstain the try to keep it to a minimum – a beer or glass of wine at the end of the week is fine but as with 'cheat' meals don't let it end up being a weekend 'session'. Again keep your goal in sight for motivation.

HYDRATION

Keeping your body well hydrated is key to helping you get lean and building muscle. Your body is made up of approx. 70% water and plays many important roles including enabling your liver to function properly which in turn detoxifies your body and rids it of any unwanted toxins. It helps lubricate joints and regulate body temperature and also works with your digestive system and improves energy levels. We constantly lose water through everyday activities so it's really important to regularly top up. Try to aim for between 2-4 litres each day. If you replace some of the teas, coffees and sugary drinks you might be used to drinking with water you'll find this target isn't so hard to reach.

We hope you enjoy our recipes. They will help make you build strong, lean muscle without adding fat. You'll feel better and look better and be on the road to building the body that you want. Good luck.

REDUCED CARB RECIPES

AVOCADO & STRAWBERRY SALAD

Ingredients

- 1 ripe avocado
- 75g/3oz strawberries, sliced
- ½ tsp paprika
- 1 shallot, finely chopped
- 2 tsp lime juice
- 1 tbsp freshly chopped coriander
- 75g/3oz watercress
- Salt & pepper to taste

Method

1 De-stone & cube the avocado.

2 Combine the cubed avocado, strawberries, paprika, shallots, lime & coriander together. Allow to sit for a few minutes to let the flavour infuse.

3 Pile onto a bed of watercress, season & serve.

NUTRITION PER SERVING

Calories:	258kcal	Fat:	21g
Carbohydrates:	17g	Protein:	5g

SERVES 1

SUPER SLOW ROASTED FETA TOMATOES

REDUCED CARB

Ingredients

- 400g/14oz ripe plum tomatoes
- ½ tsp each dried thyme & oregano
- 2 tbsp olive oil
- 2 tbsp freshly chopped parsley
- 75g/3oz feta cheese
- Salt & pepper to taste

Method

1 Preheat the oven to its absolutely lowest heat setting.

2 Place all the ingredients, except the parsley & feta cheese, in a bowl and mix well.

3 Tip the tomatoes onto a grilling rack with a tray underneath to catch the juices. Place in the preheated oven and leave to cook for approx. 5-6 hours.

4 Sprinkle with chopped parsley & crumbled feta cheese to serve.

NUTRITION PER SERVING

Calories:	509kcal	Fat:	44g
Carbohydrates:	19g	Protein:	14g

POMEGRANATE & CHICKEN SALAD

REDUCED CARB

Ingredients

- 150g/5oz chicken breast, sliced
- 1 garlic clove, crushed
- ½ tsp each paprika, cumin & coriander
- 1 tsp freshly grated ginger
- ½ red onion, sliced
- 50g/2oz spinach leaves
- 1 baby gem lettuce, shredded
- 1 tbsp each freshly chopped mint & basil

- 1 tbsp extra virgin olive oil
- ½ cucumber, sliced into ribbons (use a vegetable peeler)
- Juice and zest of ½ lemon
- ½ red chilli, deseeded and finely sliced
- Seeds of ½ ripe pomegranate
- 2 tsp coconut oil

Method

1 Gently sauté the chicken, garlic, ginger, dried herbs and spices in the coconut oil for 6-8 minutes or until the chicken is cooked through.

2 Meanwhile mix together the lemon juice, zest, pomegranate seeds, olive oil and chilli to make a dressing. Adjust the seasoning and mix well.

3 Place the sliced onion, spinach leaves, lettuce and cucumber into a bowl.

4 Toss the dressing through the leaves. Make sure the salad leaves are well coated with the dressing.

5 Lay out onto a plate, add the warm chicken pieces and sprinkle with fresh mint & basil.

NUTRITION PER SERVING

Calories:	402kcal	Fat:	26g
Carbohydrates:	12g	Protein:	31g

CHICKEN & SPINACH SAAG

REDUCED CARB

Ingredients

- 150g/5oz skinless chicken breast, cubed
- 1 onion, sliced
- 2 garlic cloves, crushed
- ½ tsp each ground ginger, coriander, turmeric & garam masala
- Pinch of chilli flakes
- 200g/7oz tinned chopped tomatoes

- 150g/5oz spinach leaves
- 3 tbsp Greek yoghurt
- Pinch salt
- 1 tbsp freshly chopped coriander
- 1 tbsp coconut oil
- Salt & pepper to taste

Method

1 Gently sauté the chicken, garlic and onions in the coconut oil for a few minutes.

2 Add the tomatoes, ground spices & salt and cook for 6-8 minutes.

3 Add the spinach, stir and cook for a further 2-3 minutes or until the chicken is cooked through and the spinach is wilted and piping hot.

4 Remove from the heat, stir through the yoghurt, sprinkle with chopped coriander and serve.

NUTRITION PER SERVING

Calories:	388kcal	Fat:	21g
Carbohydrates:	17g	Protein:	36g

SMOKED SALMON OMELETTE

REDUCED CARB

Ingredients

- 3 large free-range eggs
- 2 spring onions, thinly sliced
- 2 tbsp freshly chopped chives
- 1 tsp butter

- 50g/2oz smoked salmon, cut into strips
- 50g/2oz rocket
- Freshly ground black pepper

Method

1 Beat the eggs, spring onions and chives together in a bowl with a little freshly ground black pepper.

2 Heat a medium frying pan over a medium heat and gently melt the butter.

3 Add the egg mixture and tilt to cover the base of the pan. Cook for 2-3 minutes or until it begins to set.

4 Add the smoked salmon strips, fold the omelette in half and cook for a further minute or two.

5 Slide onto a plate and serve with the rocket piled on top.

NUTRITION PER SERVING

Calories:	393kcal	Fat:	27g
Carbohydrates:	4g	Protein:	32g

PARSLEY & PARMESAN PRAWN SPIRALS

Ingredients

- 1 large courgette/zucchini
- 1 tbsp extra virgin olive oil
- 1 garlic clove, crushed
- 2 shallots, sliced
- 200g/7oz peeled king prawns

- 1 tsp lemon juice
- 2 tbsp freshly chopped flat leaf parsley
- 1 tbsp grated Parmesan cheese
- Salt & pepper to taste

Method

1 First spiralize the courgette into thick spirals.

2 Heat the olive oil in a high-sided frying pan and gently sauté the garlic, shallots & prawns for a few minutes.

3 Add the courgette spirals and increase the heat. Stir fry for 2-3 minutes.

4 Remove from the heat. Add the lemon juice, parsley and Parmesan. Toss well, season & serve.

NUTRITION PER SERVING

Calories:	365kcal	Fat:	18g
Carbohydrates:	20g	Protein:	48g

LEMON CHICKEN FLATTIES

REDUCED CARB

Ingredients

Marinade Ingredients:
- 1 garlic clove, crushed
- 1 rosemary sprig, leaves finely chopped
- 2 sage leaves, finely chopped
- Zest of 1 lemon
- 1 tsp lemon juice
- 1 tbsp olive oil

Other Ingredients:
- 150g/5oz skinless chicken breast
- 2 tsp olive oil
- 1 tsp balsamic vinegar
- 75g/3oz bag rocket
- 1 tbsp Parmesan cheese shavings
- Fresh lemon wedges

Method

1 First flatten the chicken by placing it between 2 sheets of cling film and bashing with a rolling pin or meat mallet until it is only about ½ cm thick.

2 Place in a bowl while you make the marinade. Place all the marinade ingredients in a pestle and mortar and pound to combine. Brush this over the chicken and leave to marinade.

3 Heat the grill to a medium heat and grill the chicken breast for 5-8 minutes or until it is cooked through.

4 Whilst it's cooking combine the oil, balsamic vinegar and rocket in a large bowl.

5 Add the Parmesan shaving to the salad and serve with the chicken and lemon wedges.

NUTRITION PER SERVING

Calories:	535kcal	Fat:	31g
Carbohydrates:	12g	Protein:	54g

BROCCOLI WITH ANCHOVY DRESSING

SERVES 1

REDUCED CARB

Ingredients

- 50g/2oz tinned anchovy fillets
- 350g/12oz tenderstem broccoli
- 2 tbsp olive oil
- 1 garlic clove, crushed

- 1 onion, finely sliced
- 1 red chilli, deseeded & finely chopped
- Salt & pepper to taste

Method

1 Drain the anchovy fillets and put to one side.

2 Plunge the broccoli into a pan of salted boiling water and cook for 2 minutes. Drain and put to one side.

3 Heat the olive oil in a frying pan and gently sauté the garlic, onion, chilli, and anchovy fillets. Cook for a few minutes until the anchovies begin to break up.

4 Add the broccoli to the pan and increase the heat. Toss until well combined.

5 Check the seasoning and serve.

NUTRITION PER SERVING

Calories:	449kcal	Fat:	33g
Carbohydrates:	25g	Protein:	20g

SIMPLE CAPONATA

REDUCED CARB

Ingredients

- 1 tbsp olive oil
- 1 aubergine cubed
- 1 large courgette, cubed
- ¼ red onion, chopped
- 1 celery stalk, chopped
- 1 garlic clove, crushed
- 1 tbsp balsamic vinegar

- 1 tsp capers, chopped
- 75g/3oz ripe tomatoes, roughly chopped
- 5 black pitted olives, sliced
- 1 tbsp sultanas, roughly chopped
- 1 tbsp freshly chopped parsley
- 50g/2oz feta cheese
- Salt & pepper to taste

Method

1 Gently sauté the prepared aubergine, onions, celery and garlic in the olive oil for a few minutes until softened.

2 Add the balsamic vinegar, capers, tomatoes, olives & sultanas. Stir, cover and continue to very gently cook for 20-25 minutes or until everything is cooked through and tender.

3 Sprinkle with chopped parsley and crumbled feta to serve.

NUTRITION PER SERVING

Calories:	418kcal	28g
Carbohydrates:	25g	13g

CRAYFISH COCKTAIL

REDUCED CARB

Ingredients

- 1 tbsp crème fraîche
- 2 tsp horseradish sauce
- 1 tbsp lime juice
- 1 large avocado
- 2 baby gem lettuce, shredded
- 175g/6oz crayfish tails or shelled king prawns
- Sprinkle of cayenne pepper

Method

1 First combine together the horseradish, crème fraîche & lime juice to make a thick sauce.

2 Stone, peel and cube the avocado.

3 Gently combine together the sauce, avocado & crayfish tails.

4 Sit this onto a bed of shredded lettuce and sprinkle with cayenne pepper to serve.

NUTRITION PER SERVING

Calories:	498kcal	Fat:	35g
Carbohydrates:	18g	Protein:	42g

MESSY FETA OMELETTE

REDUCED CARB

Ingredients

- 4 large free-range eggs
- 1 tsp butter
- Small bunch spring onions, chopped

- 2 fresh tomatoes, chopped
- 50g/2oz feta cheese, crumbled
- Freshly ground black pepper

Method

1 Beat the eggs together in a bowl with a little freshly ground black pepper.

2 Heat a medium frying pan over a medium heat and gently melt the butter.

3 Add the eggs & feta and cook for a few minutes, stirring continuously until the eggs are just set.

4 Tip onto a plate and serve with the fresh tomatoes and spring onions piled on top.

NUTRITION PER SERVING

Calories:	504kcal	Fat:	33g
Carbohydrates:	13g	Protein:	33g

CEVICHE

Ingredients

- 250g/9oz haddock fillets, skinned and thinly sliced
- 120ml/½ cup lime juice
- 1 red onion, sliced into half moons
- 50g/2oz pitted green olives, finely chopped
- 1 green chilli, deseeded & finely chopped
- 125g/4oz vine ripened tomatoes, chopped
- Large bunch coriander, roughly chopped
- 2 tsp extra-virgin olive oil
- 1 tsp brown sugar

Method

1 In a large glass bowl combine together the fish, lime juice and red onions.

2 Ensure the fish is completely covered by lime juice as the lime juice will 'cook' the fish.

3 Cover with cling film and place in the fridge for 90 minutes.

4 Remove the fish and onions from the bowl, draining off the lime juice.

5 Gently combine with the olives, chilies, tomatoes, coriander, olive oil, sugar and a pinch of salt. Eat immediately.

NUTRITION PER SERVING

Calories:	428kcal	Fat:	13g
Carbohydrates:	33g	Protein:	50g

PEA & PRAWN FRITTATA

REDUCED CARB

Ingredients

- ½ onion, finely chopped
- 2 tsp olive oil
- 3 large free-range eggs
- 1 tbsp milk

- 75g/3oz cooked, peeled prawns
- 75g/3oz peas (defrosted if frozen)
- 50g/2oz mixed salad leaves

Method

1 Gently sauté the onion in a frying pan with the oil for a few minutes.

2 Beat the eggs and milk in a cup.

3 Take the pan off the heat and add eggs along with some seasoning.

4 Stir in the prawns and peas & return to a low heat for 9-12 minutes or until set (cover with a lid to ensure the top sets too).

5 Slide the frittata onto a plate and serve with the salad piled on top.

NUTRITION PER SERVING

Calories:	366kcal	Fat:	20g
Carbohydrates:	18g	Protein:	34g

GREEK EGGS

REDUCED CARB

Ingredients

- 4 eggs
- 2 tbsp chopped flat leaf parsley
- 2 tsp olive oil
- ½ red onion, sliced

- 1 beef tomato, diced
- 25g/1oz pitted black olives
- 50g/2oz feta cheese, crumbled
- Salt & pepper

Method

1 Heat the grill to high. Beat the eggs with the chopped parsley, salt & pepper.

2 Heat the oil in a frying pan and fry the onions over a high heat for a couple of mins until they start to brown.

3 Add the tomatoes and olives and cook for about 2 mins until the tomatoes begin to soften.

4 Turn the heat down to medium and pour in the eggs. Cook for a couple of minutes until they begin to set.

5 Crumble the feta cheese over the still wobbly eggs and place the pan under the grill for 4-5 mins until golden.

6 Slide onto a plate, cut into wedges & serve.

NUTRITION PER SERVING

Calories:	544kcal	Fat:	39g
Carbohydrates:	11g	Protein:	34g

...H CURRY

Ingredients

Curry Sauce Ingredients:
- 1 onion
- 2 inch piece fresh root ginger, peeled
- 1 tsp olive oil
- 2 tsp garam masala
- 1 tsp turmeric
- 1 red chilli, deseeded and finely chopped
- 400g/14oz tinned chopped tomatoes

- Large bunch of fresh coriander leaves

Other Ingredients:
- 1 tbsp butter
- 200g/7oz skinless haddock, cut into large chunks
- 200g/7oz skinless salmon, cut into large chunks

Method

1 First use a food processor to whizz together the onion and ginger.

2 Heat the oil in a frying pan, add the garam masala, turmeric, chilli, onion & ginger and cook for 5 minutes to make a curry base (add more oil if needed).

3 Add the tomatoes, coriander & seasoning and continue to cook for a few minutes whilst you deal with the fish.

4 In a separate pan melt the butter and cook the white fish for 2-3 mins until lightly browned. Place the browned fish into the curry saucepan and leave to simmer for a few minutes until the fish is cooked through and flakes easily.

5 Serve in a shallow bowl with extra chopped coriander.

NUTRITION PER SERVING

Calories:	704kcal	Fat:	25g
Carbohydrates:	31g	Protein:	96g

SUNDRIED MAYO CHICKEN FLATTIES

Ingredients

- 300g/11oz chicken breast
- 1 tsp butter
- Salt and pepper
- Small bunch of fresh basil, chopped
- 1 tbsp mayonnaise
- 4 sundried tomatoes, drained and finely chopped
- 1 garlic clove, crushed
- 50g/2oz rocket

Method

1 First flatten the chicken by placing it between 2 sheets of cling film and bashing with a rolling pin or meat mallet until it is only about ½ cm thick.

2 Melt the butter in a large frying pan over a medium heat, add the basil & chicken and cook for 3-4 minutes each side.

3 Meanwhile make the sundried mayo by combining together the mayonnaise, sundried tomatoes and garlic.

4 When the chicken is cooked. Top with the rocket and drizzle over the mayo sauce.

NUTRITION PER SERVING

Calories:	448kcal	Fat:	21g
Carbohydrates:	6g	Protein:	57g

STEAK & STILTON

REDUCED CARB

Ingredients

- 2 portobella mushrooms
- 250g/9oz fillet steak
- 25g/1oz stilton cheese
- 25g/1oz mascarpone

- 50g/2oz cherry tomatoes, halved
- 50g/2oz salad leaves
- Salt & freshly ground black pepper

Method

1 Preheat a griddle pan over a high heat and preheat your grill to medium.

2 Season the steak and mushrooms with a salt and pepper.

3 Place the mushrooms under the grill and cook for a few minutes each side.

4 Meanwhile cook the steak for 4 minutes each side in the pan (or to your liking) and add the tomatoes to the pan for the last couple of minutes.

5 Beat together the stilton & mascarpone and load this onto the mushrooms under the grill to melt and bubble (have the mushrooms underside facing up).

6 Leave the steak to rest whilst you slice the mushrooms and bubbling cheese then lay these onto the salad leaves. Place the rested steak on the plate and serve.

NUTRITION PER SERVING

Calories:	585kcal	Fat:	37g
Carbohydrates:	8g	Protein:	57g

SPICED SCRAMBLED EGGS

Ingredients

- 4 large free-range eggs
- 1 tsp butter
- 1 red onion, thinly sliced
- 1 red pepper, deseeded & sliced

- 1 red chilli, deseeded & finely sliced
- 25g/2oz spinach, chopped
- Freshly ground black pepper

Method

1 Beat the eggs together in a bowl with a little freshly ground black pepper.

2 Heat a medium frying pan over a medium heat and gently melt the butter. Sauté the onions, red pepper & chilli for a few minutes until softened.

3 Add the eggs & spinach and cook for a few minutes, stirring continuously until the eggs are just set.

4 Tip onto a plate and serve.

NUTRITION PER SERVING

Calories:	398kcal	Fat:	24g
Carbohydrates:	18g	Protein:	28g

SPICED CHICKEN SKEWERS

REDUCED CARB

Ingredients

- 300g/11oz skinless chicken breasts, cubed
- 2 tbsp curry powder
- 3 tbsp Greek yogurt
- 1 tbsp freshly chopped coriander
- 100g/3½oz cherry tomatoes
- 100g/3½oz button mushrooms

- 1 red onion, cut into wedges
- 1 baby gem lettuce, shredded
- 1 lemon cut into wedges
- Metal kebab skewers
- Coconut oil cooking spray
- Salt & pepper to taste

Method

1 Preheat the grill to medium.

2 Mix together the chicken pieces, half the yoghurt and the curry powder and leave to marinade for a few minutes.

3 Season the mushrooms, onion and tomatoes and thread in turn onto skewers along with the yoghurt coated chicken pieces. Spray with coconut oil and grill for approx. 8-12 minutes or until the chicken is cooked through (turn once halfway through cooking).

4 Serve the skewers on a plate arranged with shredded lettuce, lemon wedges and the rest of the yoghurt dolloped on the side.

NUTRITION PER SERVING

Calories:	530kcal	Fat:	17g
Carbohydrates:	29g	Protein:	72g

CHICKEN & RED CABBAGE COLESLAW

REDUCED CARB

Ingredients

- 150g/5oz skinless chicken breasts
- 1 tsp freshly chopped rosemary
- Juice and zest of ½ lemon
- Pinch dried crushed chilli flakes
- ½ fennel bulb, thinly sliced
- 200g/7oz red cabbage, finely shredded

- 2 tsp freshly chopped coriander
- 2 tsp olive oil
- 1 tbsp mayonnaise
- Coconut oil cooking spray
- Salt & pepper to taste

Method

1 Preheat the grill to a medium heat.

2 Season the chicken breasts. Sprinkle with rosemary and lemon zest, spray with the coconut oil and cook under a medium grill for 10-15 minutes or until properly cooked through.

3 Meanwhile mix together the olive oil, lemon juice, fennel and mayonnaise to make coleslaw. Slice the chicken breast thickly and diagonally. Serve with the coleslaw on the side and the coriander sprinkled over the top.

NUTRITION PER SERVING

Calories:	409kcal	Fat:	23g
Carbohydrates:	22g	Protein:	32g

SPICED MACKEREL FILLETS

REDUCED CARB

Ingredients

- 150g/5oz boned headless mackerel fillets
- 2-3 tsp curry powder
- 1 tsp coconut oil
- 1 tbsp horseradish sauce
- 1 tsp lemon juice
- 1 tsp chopped capers
- 125g/4oz spinach
- 50g/2oz soya beans
- Salt & pepper to taste

Method

1 Butterfly the mackerel to open into flat fillets. Season and rub with the curry powder.

2 Heat the oil in a pan and fry the mackerel for 3 minutes each side.

3 Meanwhile combine together the horseradish sauce, lemon juice & capers to make a dressing.

4 When the fish is cooked, wrap in foil and put to one side to keep warm. Add the spinach and soya beans to the empty pan and cook for a few minutes. Stir the dressing through the wilted spinach & beans and serve with the cooked mackerel fillets.

NUTRITION PER SERVING

Calories:	385kcal	Fat:	18g
Carbohydrates:	30g	Protein:	39g

BALSAMIC TUNA & ZUCCHINI

REDUCE CARB

Ingredients

- 2 medium courgettes
- ½ red onion, finely chopped
- 3 tsp olive oil
- 200g/7oz fresh tuna steak
- 1 tbsp balsamic vinegar
- 50g/2oz feta cheese
- 1 Iceberg lettuce, shredded
- Salt & pepper to taste

Method

1 Gently sauté the courgettes and red onion in 2 teaspoons of the olive oil for a few minutes until softened.

2 Season the tuna. Put a separate frying pan on a high heat with the rest of the olive oil and balsamic vinegar.

3 Place the tuna in the pan and cook for 2 minutes each side. Remove the tuna from the pan and arrange on the plate with the shredded lettuce and courgettes.

4 Crumble the feta cheese over the top to serve.

NUTRITION PER SERVING

| Calories: | 533kcal | Fat: | 27g |
| Carbohydrates: | 16g | Protein: | 58g |

...IED TOMATO & ...KEN SALAD

Ingredients

- 150g/5oz skinless chicken breast
- 10 cherry tomatoes
- 3 sundried tomatoes, finely chopped
- 25g/1oz Dolcelatte cheese
- ½ medium ripe avocado, peeled & stoned

- 2 tsp extra virgin olive oil
- 2 tsp cider vinegar
- 1 tbsp Greek yoghurt
- ½ tsp paprika
- 75g/3oz mixed salad leaves

Method

1 Season the chicken fillet and place under a preheated grill for 10-15 minutes or until cooked through. Slice into strips and put to one side to cool.

2 Halve the cherry tomatoes and crumble the Dolcelatte cheese.

3 Combine together the olive oil, vinegar, yoghurt & paprika to make a dressing.

4 Toss the dressing, tomatoes, sundried tomatoes, cheese & avocado together in a large bowl and serve on a bed of salad leaves with the chicken slices on top.

NUTRITION PER SERVING

Calories:	550kcal	Fat:	34g
Carbohydrates:	31g	Protein:	35g

COURGETTE SPAGHETTI & OLIVES

REDUCE CARB

Ingredients

- 1 large courgette
- 125g/4oz ripe cherry tomatoes
- 1 tbsp balsamic vinegar
- 8 pitted black olives, halved
- 1 tbsp olive oil
- 1 garlic clove, crushed

- 1 red onion, sliced
- 1 tbsp freshly chopped basil
- Pinch of dried chillies
- 200g/7oz cooked chicken breast, sliced
- Salt & pepper to taste

Method

1 First spiralize the courgette into thin spaghetti courgette noodles.

2 Dice the ripe tomatoes and place in a bowl with the balsamic vinegar and some seasoning.

3 Heat the olive oil in a high-sided frying pan and gently sauté the garlic, onions, tomatoes and olives for a few minutes.

4 Add the courgette spaghetti and increase the heat. Stir fry for 2-3 minutes. Toss well, sprinkle with freshly chopped basil and chilli.

5 Lay the cooked chicken slices over the top, season & serve.

NUTRITION PER SERVING

| Calories: | 481kcal | Fat: | 25g |
| Carbohydrates: | 21g | Protein: | 47g |

PROTEIN 'RICE'

Ingredients

- 1 red onion, chopped
- 75g/3oz green beans
- 1 garlic clove, crushed
- 1 tbsp coconut oil
- 125g/4oz cherry tomatoes, chopped
- 150g/5oz chicken breast, sliced
- 2 tsp medium curry powder
- 2 tbsp coconut cream
- 2 tbsp flat leaf parsley, chopped
- 200g/7oz cauliflower florets
- 1 tbsp chopped coriander
- Salt & pepper to taste

Method

1 Get the onions, green beans, garlic & cherry tomatoes gently cooking in a frying pan with the olive oil. Sauté for a few minutes and then add the chicken & curry powder (add a little more olive oil if needed).

2 Cook for a few minutes until the chicken is cooked thorough then stir through the coconut cream and parsley.

3 Meanwhile place the cauliflower florets in a food processor and pulse a few times until the cauliflower is the size of rice grains.

4 Place the 'rice' in a microwavable dish, cover and cook on full power for about 90 seconds minutes or until it's piping hot.

5 Tip the 'rice' into a shallow bowl. Serve the chicken and vegetables over the top sprinkled with chopped coriander.

NUTRITION PER SERVING

Calories:	491kcal	Fat:	27g
Carbohydrates:	30g	Protein:	38g

EGG MOLEE

REDUCED CARB

Ingredients

- 1 garlic clove, crushed
- 1 onion, chopped
- 75g/3oz peas
- 1 tbsp coconut oil
- 1 tbsp tomato puree
- 200g/7oz tinned chopped tomatoes
- ½ tsp each turmeric, garam masala & ground coriander

- 120ml/ ½ cup tinned coconut milk
- 4 large free-range hard-boiled eggs
- 1 tbsp freshly chopped coriander
- Salt & pepper to taste

Method

1 Gently sauté the garlic, onions & peas in the oil for a few minutes until softened.

2 Stir through the tomato puree, tinned chopped tomatoes, dried spices & coconut milk until combined. Cut the eggs in half and place yolk side up, in the coconut milk. Gently cook until warmed through.

3 When everything is piping hot, season and serve with chopped coriander over the top.

NUTRITION PER SERVING

Calories:	**721kcal**	Fat:	55g
Carbohydrates:	25g	Protein:	33g

SALMON & FENNEL

Ingredients

- 1 tbsp coconut oil
- ½ onion, sliced
- 200g/7oz fennel bulb, finely sliced
- 1 garlic clove, crushed
- 1 celery stalk, chopped
- 200g/7oz ripe plum tomatoes, roughly chopped

- 60ml/¼ cup vegetable or chicken stock
- 225g/8oz skinless, boneless salmon fillet
- 1 tbsp freshly chopped flat leaf parsley
- Salt & pepper to taste

Method

1 In a shallow saucepan gently sauté the onion, fennel, garlic & celery in the oil for a few minutes until softened.

2 Add the roughly chopped tomatoes & stock and leave to gently simmer for 10 minutes stirring occasionally.

3 Add the fish fillet and gently combine well. Cover and simmer for a further 8-10 minutes or until the fish is cooked through and the sauce has reduced.

4 Season well and serve with parsley sprinkled over the top.

NUTRITION PER SERVING

Calories:	425kcal	Fat:	16g
Carbohydrates:	28g	Protein:	46g

FRESH MINTED FISH

REDUCED CARB

Ingredients

- 225g/8oz skinless, boneless salmon fillet
- 1 garlic clove, crushed
- 1 tbsp extra virgin olive oil
- 1 tbsp freshly chopped mint
- 2 large ripe beef tomatoes, thickly sliced
- ½ red onion finely sliced into rounds
- 50g/2oz mozzarella cheese, sliced
- ½ medium avocado, de-stoned & sliced
- Salt & pepper to taste

Method

1 Preheat the grill to a medium/high heat.

2 Mix together the garlic & olive oil and brush on either side of the fish fillet. Place the fish under the grill and cook for 3-5 minutes each side or until the fillet is cooked through.

3 Meanwhile arrange the sliced tomatoes, red onion, mozzarella & avocado on the plate. Sit the cooked fish to the side of the salad and sprinkle the mint all over.

NUTRITION PER SERVING

Calories:	641kcal	Fat:	36g
Carbohydrates:	24g	Protein:	55g

PROTEIN & PINEAPPLE SKEWERS

REDUCED CARB

Ingredients

- ½ garlic clove, crushed
- 1 tbsp extra virgin olive oil
- 2 tsp lime juice
- 150g/5oz large king prawns
- 150g/5oz chicken breast, cubed

- 75g/3oz pineapple chunks
- 1 red pepper, cut into chunks
- 75g/3oz button mushrooms
- Salt & pepper to taste
- Metal skewers

Method

1 Preheat the grill to a medium/high heat.

2 Mix together the garlic, olive oil & lime juice in a bowl. Season the prawns, chicken, peppers, mushrooms & pineapple pieces and add to the bowl.

3 Combine well and skewer each piece in turn to make two large kebabs. Place under the grill and cook for 4-5 minutes each side or until the prawns are pink and cooked through.

4 Remove from the grill, season and serve.

NUTRITION PER SERVING

Calories:	512kcal	Fat:	21g
Carbohydrates:	24g	Protein:	67g

SIMPLE GRILLED TUNA

REDUCED CARB

Ingredients

- 1 fresh tuna steak weighing 175g/6oz
- 1 tbsp extra virgin olive oil
- 2 tsp lemon juice
- 1 tbsp freshly chopped marjoram

- 75g/3oz rocket & spinach leaves
- 75g/3oz vine ripened tomatoes, sliced
- 1 tbsp Parmesan shavings
- Salt & pepper to taste

Method

1 Preheat the grill to a medium/high heat.

2 Mix together the olive oil, lemon juice & marjoram and lightly brush on either side of the steak (reserving any remaining juice).

3 Place the tuna steak under the grill and cook for 2-3 minutes each side or until the tuna is cooked to your liking.

4 Remove from the grill, season and place on a plate with the green leaves and tomatoes. Drizzle any remaining juice over the top along with the Parmesan shavings.

NUTRITION PER SERVING

Calories:	394kcal	Fat:	18g
Carbohydrates:	18g	Protein:	45g

ASPARAGUS & PARMA HAM

REDUCED CARB

Ingredients

- 150g/5oz asparagus spears
- 2 tsp olive oil
- Pinch dried chilli flakes

- 1 tsp balsamic vinegar
- 4 slices Parma ham
- Salt & pepper to taste

Method

1 Preheat the grill to a medium/high heat.

2 In a bowl mix together all the ingredients, except the Parma ham, ensuring each asparagus spear is coated with oil.

3 Place under the grill and cook for 4-6 minutes each side or until cooked through.

4 Remove from the grill, season and serve immediately with the Parma ham laid over the top.

NUTRITION PER SERVING

Calories:	250kcal	Fat:	16g
Carbohydrates:	1g	Protein:	14g

PESTO CHICKEN

REDUCED CARB

Ingredients

- 150g/5oz chicken breast
- ½ red onion, thickly sliced
- 2 tsp green pesto
- 50g/2oz French beans
- 50g/2oz ripe cherry tomatoes, halved
- 1 tsp dried oregano
- 1 tsp olive oil
- Salt & pepper to taste

Method

1 Preheat the oven to 200C/400F/gas Mark 5

2 Hold the chicken breast as if you were slicing through the centre of it. Stop slicing before you cut it in half completely (this will butterfly the breast).

3 Open the chicken breast to expose the two inside parts. Spread the inside of each breast with the pesto and close the 'sandwich' back up so you are left with pesto through the centre of the chicken breast.

4 Place the chicken, onions, beans and tomatoes in a casserole dish. Season well, sprinkle with the dried oregano, brush with olive oil and cover with foil.

5 Place in the oven and leave to cook for 25-30 minutes or until the chicken is cooked through and the vegetables are tender.

6 Remove from the oven and arrange the beans, tomatoes and onions as a bed onto which you serve each pesto chicken breast.

NUTRITION PER SERVING

Calories:	425kcal	Fat:	23g
Carbohydrates:	10g	Protein:	43g

SOLE, LIME & SALSA

REDUCED CARB

Ingredients

- 1 garlic clove, crushed
- 1 tbsp olive oil
- 150g/5oz boneless, skinless sole fillets
- 2 large plum tomatoes
- ½ chopped onion
- 1 medium avocado

- 2 tbsp freshly chopped coriander
- 2 tbsp lime juice
- 50g/2oz mixed salad leaves
- Lime wedges to serve
- Salt & pepper to taste

Method

1 Mix together the garlic & olive oil and brush onto the sole fillets.

2 Heat a frying pan and gently begin to fry the fish (add a little more oil if needed).

3 Cook the sole for 2-3 minutes each side.

4 Meanwhile halve, de-stone, peel and cube the avocado.

5 Roughly chop the tomatoes and combine with the avocado, onions, chopped coriander and lime juice to make a salsa.

6 Season and serve the cooked lemon sole with the salsa, salad leaves & lime wedges.

NUTRITION PER SERVING

Calories:	530kcal	Fat:	36g
Carbohydrates:	23g	Protein:	32g

HIGHER CARB RECIPES

BREAKFAST TOWER

HIGHER CARB

Ingredients

- 2 large portabella mushrooms
- Coconut oil cooking spray
- 50g/2oz feta cheese
- 2 tsp freshly chopped chives
- 1 garlic clove, crushed

- 2 medium free-range eggs
- 1 ripe avocado, stoned and sliced
- Handful rocket leaves
- Salt & pepper to taste

Method

1 Preheat the oven grill.

2 Spray the mushrooms with oil and place them under the grill for a few minutes to cook.

3 Meanwhile mix the feta cheese, chives & garlic together with the back of a fork and spread these evenly on the underside of the mushrooms. Season well and place them back under the grill (underside up) for a few minutes or until the mushrooms are cooked through and the cheese is melted.

4 Meanwhile fill a frying pan with boiling water and break the eggs into the gently simmering pan to poach while the mushrooms cook.

5 Put the mushrooms on the plate. Arrange the rocket over the top along with the poached eggs. Finally pile the avocado slices on top and serve.

NUTRITION PER SERVING

Calories:	521 kcal	Fat:	5g
Carbohydrates:	41g	Protein:	29g

BEETROOT & AVOCADO RYVITAS

HIGHER CARB

Ingredients

- 200g steamed beetroot, cubed
- 1 tbsp cottage cheese
- 1 tsp olive oil
- 1 tsp pumpkin seeds
- ½ ripe avocado
- 2 slices Ryvita
- Salt and pepper

Method

1 Mash together the beetroot, oil and cottage cheese to make a combined topping.

2 Season with salt and pepper and pile this onto the Ryvita.

3 Slice the avocado and lay it on top.

4 Sprinkle the pumpkin seeds over the avocado and serve.

NUTRITION PER SERVING

Calories:	349kcal	Fat:	18g
Carbohydrates:	41g	Protein:	12g

BIG TUNA SALAD

HIGHER CARB

Ingredients

Dressing Ingredients
- 1 tbsp extra virgin olive oil
- 1 tsp red wine vinegar
- 1 tsp Dijon mustard
- Freshly ground black pepper

Salad Ingredients
- 100g/3½oz green beans, halved
- 2 large hard boiled free-range eggs
- 400g/14oz tinned cannellini beans in water, drained and rinsed
- 6 cherry tomatoes, halved
- ½ red onion, finely chopped
- 150g/5oz tinned tuna steak in water, drained
- 1 romaine lettuce, shredded

Method

1 Combine together the salad dressing ingredients.

2 Steam the green beans for a few minutes (they should still be firm) and cool them quickly in a bowl of cold water.

3 Sit the shredded lettuce on a plate, add the green beans, cannellini beans, cherry tomatoes and red onions.

4 Flake the tuna on top and quarter the hard-boiled eggs. Add to the salad, drizzle with dressing and serve.

NUTRITION PER SERVING

Calories:	773kcal	Fat:	32g
Carbohydrates:	62g	Protein:	69g

DRESSED BROCCOLI

HIGHER CARB

Ingredients

- 4 medium free-range eggs
- 250g/9oz tenderstem broccoli
- 2 tbsp lemon juice
- 1 tbsp olive oil

- 1 tbsp clear honey
- 1 tbsp capers
- 2 tbsp chopped fresh mixed herbs
- Salt and freshly ground pepper

Method

1 Steam the broccoli for a few minutes (it should still be firm) and cool quickly in a bowl of cold water.

2 Mix the lemon juice, oil, honey, capers and herbs together in a cup to make a dressing.

3 Shell the eggs and chop.

4 Add the broccoli to a bowl and toss with the dressing.

5 Gently combine with the chopped eggs. Season with salt & pepper and serve.

NUTRITION PER SERVING

| Calories: | 568kcal | Fat: | 34g |
| Carbohydrates: | 39g | Protein: | 33g |

COD & CHUNKY SALSA

HIGHER CARB

Ingredients

- 1 tsp lime juice
- 1 tsp white wine vinegar
- 10 cherry tomatoes, diced
- 3 spring onions, finely chopped
- 1 medium avocado, peeled & stoned
- 1 garlic clove, crushed

- 1 tbsp olive oil
- 75g/3oz asparagus spears
- 200g/7oz boneless, skinless cod fillet
- 50g/2oz watercress
- Salt & pepper to taste

Method

1 Pre-heat the grill to a medium setting.

2 Combine together the lime juice, vinegar, cherry tomatoes, spring onions and avocado to create a chunky salsa.

3 Mix together the garlic & olive oil and brush onto the cod fillet & asparagus spears.

4 Place the fish and asparagus under a preheated grill and cook for 6-9 minutes or until the cod is cooked through and the asparagus spears are tender

5 Season and serve the cooked cod with the salsa over the top and the watercress on the side of the plate.

NUTRITION PER SERVING

Calories:	649kcal	Fat:	39g
Carbohydrates:	36g	Protein:	41g

PORK STIR FRY

HIGHER CARB

Ingredients

- 150g/5oz pork tenderloin, sliced
- 1 yellow pepper, deseeded & sliced
- 1 bunch spring onions, sliced lengthways into strips
- 1 garlic clove, crushed
- 2 tsp freshly grated ginger
- 1 tbsp soy sauce

- 1 tbsp mirin/rice wine
- 50g/2oz baby sweetcorn
- 200g/7oz beansprouts & shredded vegetables
- 2 tsp coconut oil
- Salt & pepper to taste

Method

1 Gently sauté the pork, onions, peppers & garlic in the coconut oil for a few minutes.

2 Increase the heat and add all the other ingredients. Stir fry for 3-5 minutes or until the pork is cooked through and everything is well coated with the mirin and soy.

3 Season and serve.

NUTRITION PER SERVING

Calories:	380kcal	Fat:	18g
Carbohydrates:	46g	Protein:	43g

SHREDDED CHICKEN & LEEK SOUP

HIGHER CARB

Ingredients

- 125g/4oz sweet potatoes
- 2 leeks
- 125g/4oz cooked chicken breast
- 1 tbsp coconut oil

- 1 tsp dried mixed herbs
- 500ml/2 cups chicken stock
- Salt & pepper to taste

Method

1 Chop up the potatoes (no need to peel), slice the leeks and shred the chicken with two forks.

2 Heat the oil in a saucepan and add the leeks, potatoes & mixed herbs. Sauté for a few minutes and then add the stock.

3 Turn up the heat, bring to the boil and simmer for 7-10 minutes or until the potatoes are soft.

4 Blend to a smooth consistency and return to the pan.

5 Add the shredded chicken and heat through for a minute or two.

6 Check the seasoning and serve.

NUTRITION PER SERVING

Calories:	418kcal	Fat:	16g
Carbohydrates:	42g	Protein:	27g

MUSTARD MUSHROOMS ON RYE

HIGHER CARB

Ingredients

- 2 tsp coconut oil
- ½ garlic clove, crushed
- 2 shallots, sliced
- 150g/5oz mushrooms, sliced
- 2 tsp Dijon mustard

- 2 tbsp crème fraiche
- 50g/2oz spinach
- 2 slices natural rye bread, lightly toasted
- 1 tbsp freshly chopped flat leaf parsley
- Salt & pepper to taste

Method

1 Gently heat the oil in a pan and sauté the shallots and garlic for a few minutes. Add the mushrooms and continue cooking for 8-10 minutes or until the mushrooms are soft and cooked through.

2 Stir through the mustard and crème fraiche along with the spinach, combine well and warm through until the spinach is wilted.

3 Pile the creamy mushrooms & spinach onto the rye toast and sprinkle with chopped parsley. Season and serve.

NUTRITION PER SERVING

Calories:	393kcal	Fat:	21g
Carbohydrates:	42g	Protein:	10g

WHOLEMEAL BERRY PANCAKES

HIGHER CARB

Ingredients

- 50g/2oz wholemeal plain flour
- 1 large free-range egg
- 120ml/½ cup milk
- 1 tsp olive oil

- 1 tsp butter
- 75g/3oz raspberries
- 1 tbsp Greek yoghurt

Method

1 Beat the egg, milk and oil together in a cup and slowly add to the flour, stirring until you have a smooth batter (or just blitz it all in the blender)

2 Heat a large nonstick frying pan on a medium heat and melt the butter. Allow 2-3 tablespoons of pancake mixture for each pancake.

3 Cook the pancakes for 1-2 minutes, or until the underside is lightly browned. Turn over and cook the other side for a further minute.

4 Top the pancakes with the mixed berries and yoghurt to serve.

NUTRITION PER SERVING

Calories:	419kcal	Fat:	18g
Carbohydrates:	42g	Protein:	17g

FRENCH TOAST

HIGHER CARB

Ingredients

- 120ml/½ cup milk
- 3 large free-range eggs
- ½ tsp ground cinnamon
- 1 scoop protein powder
- 3 pieces thick wholemeal bread

- 1 banana
- 1 tbsp walnut halves, chopped
- 1 tsp honey
- Coconut oil spray

Method

1 Whisk the eggs, milk, cinnamon & protein powder together in a cup and pour this onto a plate.

2 Soak each slice of bread in the egg mixture.

3 Coat a pan in coconut oil spray, heat and fry the bread for 2 minutes each side, or until golden brown.

4 Top with sliced banana, chopped walnut halves and a drizzle of honey.

NUTRITION PER SERVING

Calories:	755kcal	Fat:	18g
Carbohydrates:	83g	Protein:	51g

KALE OATS

HIGHER CARB

Ingredients

- 75g/3oz rolled oats
- 300ml/10½floz milk
- 1 large free-range egg
- 2 fresh tomatoes, chopped
- 50g/2oz spinach

- 50g/2oz kale
- 1 garlic clove, crushed
- 1 tbsp goat's cheese
- Coconut oil spray

Method

1 Cook the oats in a saucepan with the milk for a few minutes.

2 Meanwhile heat a non-stick pan with some coconut oil spray and add the garlic and kale. Stir and cook for a minute or two.

3 Add the spinach and chopped tomatoes and keep stirring for a minute. Push the veggies to the side and fry the egg until cooked.

4 Sit the goats cheese on top of the veggies to melt. When everything is cooked place the porridge in a bowl add everything on top and serve.

NUTRITION PER SERVING

Calories:	554kcal	Fat:	17g
Carbohydrates:	72g	Protein:	33g

CHICKEN QUINOA SALAD

HIGHER CARB

Ingredients

- 125g/4oz cooked chicken breast
- 1 tsp olive oil
- ½ garlic clove, crushed
- 1 tbsp Greek yoghurt
- 2 tsp lemon juice

- 200g/7oz cooked quinoa, left to cool
- 1 tbsp chopped fresh mint
- 1 tbsp chopped coriander
- Small bunch spring onions, chopped
- ½ ripe mango, peeled & diced

Method

1 Slice the cooked chicken breast.

2 Combine together the oil, garlic, yoghurt and lemon juice to make a creamy dressing.

3 Gently combine together all the other ingredients and fluff with a fork.

4 Sit the chicken breast on top, dollop the yoghurt dressing over and serve.

NUTRITION PER SERVING

Calories:	677kcal	Fat:	17g
Carbohydrates:	86g	Protein:	54g

CHICKEN WHOLEMEAL WRAP

SERVES 1

HIGHER CARB

Ingredients

- 150g/5oz skinless chicken breasts, cubed
- 1 garlic clove, crushed
- ½ onion, chopped
- ½ red pepper, deseeded & chopped
- 1 tbsp soy sauce
- 1 tsp honey
- 1 tsp tomato puree/paste
- ½ tsp each mustard powder & ground ginger
- 2 tsp Greek yoghurt
- Handful of shredded lettuce
- 1 wholemeal wrap
- 1 large ripe tomato, chopped
- Coconut oil cooking spray
- Salt & pepper to taste

Method

1 Mix together the garlic, soy sauce, honey, tomato puree and ground spices. Add the chicken pieces and combine really well.

2 Sauté the coated chicken, onions and peppers in a little coconut oil for 8-10 minutes or until the chicken is cooked through and the peppers are softened.

3 Pile on top of the wrap, add the lettuce, chopped tomatoes and the yoghurt. Roll tightly and serve.

NUTRITION PER SERVING

Calories:	518kcal	Fat:	13g
Carbohydrates:	53g	Protein:	53g

CARDOMOM COUSCOUS

HIGHER CARB

Ingredients

- 150g/5oz chicken breast
- 1 tbsp lemon juice
- ½ tsp each ground cumin, turmeric, cinnamon & coriander
- 1 black cardamom pod
- 1 garlic clove, crushed

- 100g/3½oz tinned chickpeas, drained
- 300g/11oz tinned chopped tomatoes
- 1 tbsp freshly chopped coriander
- 50g/2oz wholemeal giant couscous
- 1 chicken stock cube

Method

1 Preheat the oven to 200C/400F/Gas Mark 6.

2 Bash the cardamom pods open and grind the seeds with a pestle and mortar. Place all the ingredients (except the couscous, stock cube & chopped coriander) in a small ovenproof dish. Combine well, season, cover and cook for 20-25 minutes in the preheated oven - or until the chicken is cooked through.

3 Meanwhile cook the couscous in boiling water along with the crumbled stock cube until tender.

4 Use two forks to shred the chicken, then load this (and the juices from the dish) over the top of the couscous.

5 Sprinkle the chopped coriander over the top to serve.

NUTRITION PER SERVING

Calories:	531kcal	Fat:	31g
Carbohydrates:	67g	Protein:	9g

CHICKEN & SWEET POTATO CHOWDER

SERVES 1

HIGHER CARB

Ingredients

- 125g/4oz skinless chicken breasts, diced
- 150g/5oz sweet potatoes, peeled & diced
- ½ onion, chopped
- 1 garlic clove, crushed
- 500ml/2 cups chicken stock
- 75g/3oz frozen sweetcorn
- 25g/1oz spinach
- 60ml/¼ cup single cream
- 1 tbsp freshly chopped flat leaf parsley
- 2 tsp coconut oil
- Salt & pepper to taste

Method

1 Gently sauté the chicken, onions & garlic in the oil for 4-5 minutes.

2 Add all the ingredients, except the chopped parsley & spinach, to a saucepan and gently simmer for 8-10 minutes or until the potatoes are tender and the chicken is cooked through. Stir through the spinach until wilted and the cream until warmed through.

3 Season and serve with parsley sprinkled over the top.

NUTRITION PER SERVING

Calories:	693kcal	Fat:	38g
Carbohydrates:	50g	Protein:	38g

LIME CHICKEN PITTA

HIGHER CARB

Ingredients

- **125g/4oz skinless chicken breasts, cubed**
- **1 tbsp lime juice**
- **½ tsp white wine vinegar**
- **½ tsp coarse sea salt**
- **½ tsp honey**
- **1 baby gem lettuce, finely shredded**
- **1 tsp freshly chopped flat leaf parsley**
- **1 large wholemeal pitta bread**
- **Coconut oil cooking spray**
- **2 tsp Greek yoghurt**
- **Pinch cayenne pepper**
- **Salt & pepper to taste**

Method

1 Place the chicken pieces in a bowl with the lime, vinegar, honey and salt. Refrigerate and leave to marinate for an hour or two.

2 Pat dry, spray with coconut oil and cook under a medium grill for 6-8 minutes or until properly cooked through.

3 Split the pitta bread and pile the chicken, shredded lettuce and a dollop of yogurt inside and a pinch of cayenne pepper on top.

NUTRITION PER SERVING

Calories:	420kcal	Fat:	8g
Carbohydrates:	39g	Protein:	33g

CHICKEN & PINEAPPLE STIR FRY

HIGHER CARB

Ingredients

- 2 tbsp soy sauce
- 2 tsp smooth peanut butter
- 1 tsp honey
- ½ tsp Tabasco sauce
- ½ tsp rice vinegar
- 1 garlic clove, crushed
- 150g/5oz skinless chicken breasts, sliced
- 150g/5oz straight to wok wholemeal noodles
- 125g/4oz beansprouts and shredded vegetables
- 75g/3oz tinned pineapple, drained and cubed
- ½ onion, sliced
- 1 tbsp freshly chopped flat leaf parsley.
- 1 tsp coconut oil
- Salt & pepper to taste

Method

1 First make the stir fry sauce by combining together the soy sauce, peanut butter, honey, Tabasco, vinegar and half the garlic.

2 Meanwhile season and gently sauté the chicken, onion and the rest of the garlic in the coconut oil for a few minutes.

3 Add the noodles, pineapple, sauce and beansprouts. Turn up the heat and stir-fry until everything is cooked through and piping hot. Sprinkle with freshly chopped parsley and serve.

NUTRITION PER SERVING

Calories:	715kcal	Fat:	17g
Carbohydrates:	89g	Protein:	52g

LEMONGRASS LAKSA

HIGHER CARB

Ingredients

- 150g/5oz skinless chicken breast, chopped
- ½ onion, chopped
- 1 red chilli, deseeded & finely chopped
- 50g/2oz spinach, chopped
- ½ tsp ground ginger
- 1 tsp turmeric
- 1 tbsp freshly chopped coriander
- 1 lemongrass stalk, finely chopped

- 500ml/2 cups chicken stock
- 120ml/½ cup coconut milk
- 2 tsp fish sauce
- 50g/2oz dried wholemeal noodles
- 1 lime wedge
- 1 tsp coconut oil
- Salt & pepper to taste

Method

1 Gently sauté the onions, chopped lemongrass and chillies in the coconut oil for a few minutes.

2 Add all the other ingredients, except the coconut milk and lime juice, to the pan and leave to cook for 8-10 minutes or until the chicken is cooked through and the noodles are tender.

3 Stir through the coconut milk and serve with a lime wedge.

NUTRITION PER SERVING

Calories:	739kcal	Fat:	33g
Carbohydrates:	51g	Protein:	59g

CHICKEN & WATERCRESS RISOTTO

HIGHER CARB

Ingredients

- 150g/5oz skinless chicken breast, chopped
- 1 tbsp olive oil
- 1 tsp butter
- 1 onion, chopped
- 1 garlic clove, crushed

- 75g/3oz Arborio risotto rice
- 500ml/2 cups chicken stock
- 125g/4oz frozen peas
- 75g/3oz watercress
- Salt & pepper to taste

Method

1 Sauté the chicken, onion and garlic in the oil and butter for a few minutes. Add the risotto to the pan and make sure each grain is coated well with the oil & butter.

2 Gradually add the stock, a ladle at a time, stirring and making sure the liquid is absorbed before adding the next ladle. After 10 minutes of cooking add the peas.

3 Cook until the risotto is tender (about 20 -25minutes), add a little more or less stock if needed.

4 Remove from the heat, season, stir through the watercress and serve immediately.

NUTRITION PER SERVING

Calories:	771kcal	Fat:	23g
Carbohydrates:	81g	Protein:	43g

CHICKPEA PRAWN RICE BOWL

HIGHER CARB

Ingredients

- 1 tbsp coconut oil
- ½ onion, sliced
- 1 garlic clove, crushed
- ½ red chilli, deseeded & finely chopped
- 100g/3½oz ripe plum tomatoes, roughly chopped
- 150g/5oz tinned chickpeas, drained
- 150g/5oz peeled raw king prawns
- 2 tsp lemon juice
- 1 tbsp freshly chopped parsley
- 150g/5oz microwavable brown rice
- Lemon wedges to serve
- Salt & pepper to taste

Method

1 Heat the coconut oil in a pan and gently sauté the onion, garlic & chilli for a few minutes until softened.

2 Add the roughly chopped tomatoes & chickpeas and leave to gently simmer for 15 minutes stirring occasionally.

3 Add the prawns & lemon juice and combine well. Cover and simmer for a further 10 minutes or until the prawns are pink and cooked through.

4 Toss the cooked rice into the pan.

5 Sprinkle with chopped basil and serve with lemon wedges.

NUTRITION PER SERVING

Calories:	635kcal	Fat:	18g
Carbohydrates:	80g	Protein:	38g

PRAWN & FETA SPAGHETTI

HIGHER CARB

Ingredients

- 150g/5oz shelled king prawns
- 1 garlic clove, crushed
- ½ onion, chopped
- 2 tsp coconut oil
- 75g/3oz whole wheat spaghetti
- 1 tbsp lemon juice
- 1 tbsp extra virgin olive oil
- 25g/1oz rocket leaves
- 25g/1oz feta cheese
- Salt & pepper to taste

Method

1 Cook the spaghetti in salted boiling water until tender.

2 Meanwhile season and gently sauté the prawns, onions & garlic in the coconut oil for a few minutes until the prawns are cooked through.

3 Add the drained pasta to the pan along with the olive oil and lemon juice & toss well.

4 Remove from the heat, tip into a bowl and pile the rocket on top.

5 Crumble the feta cheese over the rocket, season and serve.

NUTRITION PER SERVING

Calories:	663kcal	Fat:	32g
Carbohydrates:	51g	Protein:	39g

RYE & PESTO CRUSTED SALMON

HIGHER CARB

Ingredients

- 50g/2oz bulgur wheat
- 1 vegetable stock cube
- 200g/7oz boneless, skinless salmon fillet
- 1 tbsp green pesto

- 1 tbsp fresh rye breadcrumbs
- 200g/7oz tenderstem broccoli
- Lemon wedge to serve
- Salt & pepper to taste

Method

1 Preheat the grill to a medium setting.

2 Cook the bulgur wheat in boiling water along with the crumbled stock cube for 15 minutes or until tender.

3 Meanwhile season the salmon fillet. Mix the pesto & breadcrumbs together and coat the top of the salmon fillet with the breadcrumb mixture.

4 Place the salmon under a preheated grill and cook for 10-15 minutes or until the salmon fillets are cooked through.

5 Whilst the salmon is cooking plunge the broccoli into salted boiling water and cook for a 2-3 minutes or until just tender.

6 Drain any excess liquid from the bulgur wheat and fluff with a fork. Drain the broccoli and serve with the salmon fillet, bulgur wheat and lemon wedge.

NUTRITION PER SERVING

Calories:	589kcal	Fat:	18g
Carbohydrates:	57g	Protein:	59g

WILD RICE & CHICKEN CASHEW

HIGHER CARB

Ingredients

- 125g/4oz skinless chicken breast, sliced
- 125g/4oz tenderstem broccoli
- 75g/3oz wild rice
- 2 tsp coconut oil
- 1 garlic clove, crushed
- ½ onion, chopped
- 2 tsp soy sauce

- 60ml/ ¼ cup chicken stock
- 1 tsp fish sauce
- 200g/7oz spinach leaves, chopped
- 1 fresh lime wedge
- 10 cashew nuts, chopped
- Salt & pepper to taste

Method

1 Season the chicken and roughly chop the broccoli.

2 Place the wild rice in salted boiling water and cook for 40-50 minutes or until tender.

3 Meanwhile heat the oil in a frying pan and gently sauté the garlic and onions for a few minutes.

4 Add the chicken & chopped broccoli to the pan along with the soy sauce, chicken stock & fish sauce. Stir-fry for 8-10 minutes or until the chicken is cooked through.

5 Add the drained rice to the frying pan along with the spinach.

6 Combine for a minute or two, pile into a bowl with the nuts sprinkled over the top and the lime wedge on the side. Check the seasoning and serve.

NUTRITION PER SERVING

Calories:	738kcal	Fat:	22g
Carbohydrates:	77g	Protein:	65g

SERVES 1

QUINOA CITRUS CHICKEN

Ingredients

- 50g/2oz quinoa
- 1 vegetable stock cube
- 1 tbsp sultanas, chopped
- 175g/6oz skinless chicken breast
- 1 shallot, chopped
- 1 garlic clove, crushed

- 2 tsp lemon juice
- 1 tbsp olive oil
- Lemon wedges to serve
- 1 tbsp freshly chopped coriander
- Salt & pepper to taste

Method

1 Cook the quinoa in the boiling water with the vegetable stock cube for 15-20 minutes or until tender. Add the sultanas for the last few 2 minutes of cooking. Drain the quinoa and put to one side.

2 Meanwhile season the chicken breast meat. Grill for 15-20 mins or until cooked through and leave to cool before roughly chopping.

3 Gently sauté the chopped shallot, garlic, & lemon juice in the olive oil for a few minutes and add the chicken.

4 Fluff the quinoa with a fork and pile into the shallot pan. Mix well and serve with fresh lemon wedges on the side and chopped coriander sprinkled over the top.

NUTRITION PER SERVING

Calories:	521kcal	Fat:	22g
Carbohydrates:	28g	Protein:	52g

SWEET & HOT PRAWNS

HIGHER CARB

Ingredients

- 75g/3oz brown rice
- 1 tbsp extra virgin olive oil
- 1 red onion
- 75g/3oz green beans, chopped
- 2 garlic cloves, crushed
- 1 birds eye chilli, sliced (leave the seeds in)
- 2 tbsp lime juice

- 2 tbsp fish sauce
- ½ tsp brown sugar
- 175g/6oz cooked prawns, chopped
- 1 tbsp flat leaf parsley, chopped
- 50g/2oz spinach
- Salt & pepper to taste

Method

1 Cook the rice in salted boiling water until tender, then drain.

2 Meanwhile heat up a frying pan with the olive oil and sauté the onions for a few minutes until softened

3 While the onions are cooking combine the garlic cloves, chilli, lime juice, fish sauce and brown sugar to make a spicy, sweet & sour dressing.

4 Tip the drained rice and prawns into the pan with the onions and warm for a few minutes until everything is piping hot. Add the spinach for the last 60 seconds until it is gently wilted.

5 Tip the prawns & rice into a shallow bowl, drizzle the dressing over the top and sprinkle with parsley.

NUTRITION PER SERVING

Calories:	564kcal	Fat:	19g
Carbohydrates:	63g	Protein:	37g

VEGGIE WHOLEWHEAT SALAD

HIGHER CARB

Ingredients

- 50g/2oz giant whole wheat couscous
- 1 tbsp olive oil
- 1 garlic clove, crushed
- 1 red pepper, sliced
- ½ aubergine, cubed
- ½ red onion, chopped
- 12 cherry tomatoes, halved
- 50g/2oz spinach leaves
- 50g/2oz feta cheese
- Salt & pepper to taste

Method

1 Prepare the couscous according to the instructions on the packet.

2 Mix the olive oil, garlic, peppers, aubergine, onions and tomatoes in a bowl. Add to a frying pan and gently sauté for 8-10 minutes or until all the vegetables are tender and cooked through.

3 Add the cooked couscous & spinach to the pan and combine well.

4 Pile everything on a plate on top of the spinach, crumble over the feta cheese. Season and serve.

NUTRITION PER SERVING

Calories:	588kcal	Fat:	29g
Carbohydrates:	73g	Protein:	20g

VEGGIE LENTIL SALAD

HIGHER CARB

SERVES 1

Ingredients

- 200g/7oz cooked tinned lentils
- 200g/7oz shelled fresh broad beans
- 1 tbsp olive oil
- 3 anchovy fillets, drained
- ½ garlic clove, crushed
- 2 shallots, sliced
- 150g/5oz ripe plum tomatoes, roughly chopped
- 1 tbsp freshly chopped oregano
- 50g/2oz rocket
- Salt & pepper to taste

Method

1 Place the broad beans in a pan of boiling water, cook for 2 minutes and drain.

2 Meanwhile heat the olive oil in a high-sided frying pan and gently sauté the anchovy fillets, garlic, onions, chopped tomatoes and oregano. Once cooked, leave to cool.

3 Drain the lentils and toss well with the cooled tomato mix.

4 Pile on top of a bed of rocket and serve.

NUTRITION PER SERVING

Calories:	616kcal	Fat:	17g
Carbohydrates:	81g	Protein:	33g

GINGER PORK & PINEAPPLE

HIGHER CARB

Ingredients

- 125g/4oz pork tenderloin
- ½ red chilli, deseeded & finely chopped
- 2 tbsp rice wine vinegar
- Pinch of brown sugar
- 1 tbsp soy sauce
- 75g/3oz brown rice

- 1 tsp olive oil
- ½ onion, sliced
- 1 tbsp freshly grated ginger
- 75g/3oz tinned pineapple chunks, drained
- Salt & pepper to taste

Method

1 Season and thinly slice the pork. Place in a bowl with the chopped chilli, vinegar, brown sugar & soy sauce. Combine well and leave to marinade for 15-20 minutes.

2 Cook the brown rice in salted boiling water until tender.

3 Meanwhile heat the olive oil and gently stir-fry the onions & ginger for a few minutes until softened.

4 Increase the heat and add the marinated pork & pineapples chunks. Stir-fry until the sauce thickens up and the dish is piping hot.

5 Serve with the drained brown rice.

NUTRITION PER SERVING

Calories:	470kcal	Fat:	9g
Carbohydrates:	67g	Protein:	31g

LAMB KOFTA

HIGHER CARB

Ingredients

- 150g/5oz lean lamb mince
- ½ tsp each ground cumin, salt & coriander
- 1 garlic clove, crushed
- 1 tsp olive oil
- 1 wholemeal pitta bread

- 1 baby gem lettuce, shredded
- 1 tbsp Greek yoghurt
- 1 tsp mint sauce
- 2 kebab skewers
- Salt & pepper to taste

Method

1 Preheat the grill.

2 Place the lamb mince, cumin, coriander, garlic & salt in a food processor and pulse to combine. Scoop out the mixture and use your hands to form into 2 balls.

3 Roll the balls into oval shapes and thread lengthways onto the skewers. Spray with a brush with olive oil, place under a preheated medium grill and cook for 8-12 minutes or until cooked through.

4 Mix the yoghurt and mint sauce together.

5 Warm the pitta bread under the grill, take the koftas off the skewers and place in the pittas along with the shredded lettuce & mint yoghurt.

NUTRITION PER SERVING

Calories:	554kcal	Fat:	31g
Carbohydrates:	31g	Protein:	34g

HOMEMADE MUESLI

SERVES 1

HIGHER CARB

Ingredients

- 75g/3oz rolled oats
- 1 tbsp sultanas
- 1 tbsp almond flakes
- 25g/1oz dried chopped apricots
- 120ml/½ cup pure apple juice

- 1 green apple
- 1 tbsp Greek yoghurt
- ½ banana
- 1 tbsp honey

Method

1 Combine together the oats, sultanas, almond flakes, apricots and apple juice. Mix well and put to one side to soak for 10 minutes.

2 Meanwhile peel and grate the apple. Peel & slice the banana.

3 After 10 minutes check the apple juice has soaked into the oats and fruit.

4 Place in a bowl and cover with the grated apple.

5 Dollop a tablespoon of Greek yoghurt on top and arrange the banana slices in a mound on the yoghurt.

6 Drizzle the honey over the top and serve immediately.

NUTRITION PER SERVING

Calories:	**587kcal**	Fat:	**12g**
Carbohydrates:	**116g**	Protein:	**11g**

GARLIC GNOCCHI & ROCKET

HIGHER CARB

Ingredients

- 250g/9oz gnocchi
- 1 tbsp olive oil
- 1 garlic clove, crushed

- 50g/2oz rocket
- 125g/4oz cooked chicken breast
- Salt & pepper to taste

Method

1 Shred the chicken with two forks

2 Place the gnocchi in a pan of salted boiling water.

3 Cook for 2-3 minutes or until the gnocchi begins to float to the top.

4 Meanwhile gently heat the olive oil in a saucepan and sauté the garlic & shredded chicken.

5 As soon as the gnocchi is cooked, drain and place in the frying pan with the olive oil and garlic.

6 Move the gnocchi around for a minute or two to coat each dumpling in the garlic oil.

7 Add the rocket to the pan, quickly toss and serve.

NUTRITION PER SERVING

Calories:	627kcal	Fat:	18g
Carbohydrates:	73g	Protein:	40g

SMOOTHIES SNACKS & TREATS

CARB KIWI SMOOTHIE

BODY BUILDING

—— Ingredients ——

- 2 peeled kiwi fruit
- ½ mango, peeled, stoned and chopped
- 120ml/ ½ cup pineapple juice
- 120ml/ ½ cup water
- ½ banana, sliced

NUTRITION PER SERVING

Calories:	308kcal	Fat:	2g
Carbohydrates:	76g	Protein:	4g

—— Method ——

Place all the ingredients in a blender and whizz until smooth. Add a handful of ice to the blender if you want a slushie type shake.

BODY BUILDING

BLUEBERRY YOG SMOOTHIE

NUTRITION PER SERVING

Calories:	361kcal	Fat:	9g
Carbohydrates:	40g	Protein:	39g

—— Ingredients ——

- 250ml/1 cup unsweetened almond milk
- 125g/4oz blueberries
- 2 tbsp Greek yoghurt
- 2 scoops vanilla flavoured protein powder

—— Method ——

Place all the ingredients in a blender and whizz until smooth. Add a little water or coconut milk if you prefer a 'longer' drink or you may wish to add handful of ice to make this a super slushie.

CHOCOLATE NUT SMOOTHIE

SERVES 1

NUTRITION PER SERVING

Calories: **467kcal** Fat: **25g**
Carbohydrates: **27g** Protein: **45g**

— Ingredients —

- 250ml/1 cup unsweetened almond milk
- 2 scoops chocolate flavoured protein powder
- 1 tbsp almond butter
- 5 cashew nuts

— Method —

Place all the ingredients in a blender and whizz until smooth. If you have a nutribullet type blender this will blend the cashew nuts in seconds. If not you may need to whizz repeatedly until you get the consistency you are after.

SERVES 1

OATIE ALMOND GREEN SMOOTHIE

BODY BUILDING

— Ingredients —

- 250ml/1 cup almond unsweetened milk
- 2 scoops vanilla flavoured protein
- 1 apple, peeled & cored
- 50g/2oz spinach

NUTRITION PER SERVING

Calories: **607kcal** Fat: **18g**
Carbohydrates: **75g** Protein: **39g**

— Method —

Place all the ingredients in a blender and whizz until smooth. If you have a nutribullet type blender you don't need to bother peeling the apple, if not your blender may not handle the peel very well so go ahead and peel it when you core the apple.

CRANBERRY CARB BALLS

BODY BUILDING

Ingredients

- 150g/5oz dried figs
- 150g/5oz almonds
- 150g/5oz dried cranberries

- ½ tsp each ground cinnamon & ginger
- 2 tbsp orange juice

Method

1 Add all the ingredients to a food processor and pulse repeatedly until the ingredients are finely chopped and combined.

2 Wet your hands and divide the mixture into 15 even portions.

3 Roll each portion in to energy balls. Cover and chill for a couple of hours before eating.

NUTRITION PER BALL

Calories:	111kcal	Fat:	5g
Carbohydrates:	16g	Protein:	2g

GRANOLA SNACK BITES

BODY BUILDING

Ingredients

- 2 tbsp ground almonds
- 2 tbsp raisins
- 125g/4oz blueberries
- 2 tbsp honey

- 1 tbsp coconut oil
- 100g/3½oz rolled oats
- 75g/3oz pumpkin seeds
- 1 tsp ground cinnamon

Method

1 Add all the ingredients to a food processor and pulse repeatedly until the ingredients are finely chopped and combined.

2 Wet your hands and divide the mixture into 15 even portions.

3 Roll each portion in to energy balls. Cover and chill for a couple of hours before eating.

NUTRITION PER BALL

Calories:	103kcal	Fat:	5g
Carbohydrates:	13g	Protein:	3g

NUTTY BANANA BITES

Ingredients

- 175g/6oz crunchy peanut butter
- 1 large banana
- 150g/5oz pitted dates

- 1 tbsp ground almonds
- 2 tbsp raisins
- 3 tbsp coconut flakes

Method

1 Add all the ingredients, except the coconut flakes, to a food processor and pulse repeatedly until the ingredients are finely chopped and combined.

2 Wet your hands and divide the mixture into 15 even portions.

3 Roll each portion in to energy balls.

4 Scatter the coconut flakes on a plate and roll the balls into the flakes to cover.

5 Cover and chill for a couple of hours before eating.

NUTRITION PER BALL

Calories:	163kcal	Fat:	7g
Carbohydrates:	24g	Protein:	4g

CARROT SNACK BALLS

Ingredients

- 150g/5oz rolled oats
- 2 tbsp coconut flour
- 4oz/125g pitted dates
- 1 carrot, peeled & grated

- ½ tsp ground cinnamon
- Pinch of nutmeg
- 1 tbsp orange juice
- 3 tbsp coconut flakes

Method

1 Add all the ingredients, except the coconut flakes, to a food processor and pulse repeatedly until the ingredients are finely chopped and combined.

2 Wet your hands and divide the mixture into 15 even portions.

3 Roll each portion in to energy balls.

4 Scatter the coconut flakes on a plate and roll the balls into the flakes to cover.

5 Cover and chill for a couple of hours before eating.

NUTRITION PER BALL

Calories:	90kcal	Fat:	2g
Carbohydrates:	19g	Protein:	2g

 **RY BITES**

Ingredients

- 125g/4oz rolled oats
- 2 tbsp crunchy peanut butter
- 75g/3oz dried cherries, chopped
- 2 tbsp sunflower seeds, chopped
- 1 tbsp water
- 2 tbsp honey

Method

1 Add all the ingredients to a bowl and combine really well with a large wooden spoon. Cover and leave to chill for 30 minutes.

2 Wet your hands and divide the mixture into 15 even portions.

3 Roll each portion in to energy balls. Cover and chill for a couple of hours before eating.

NUTRITION PER BALL

Calories:	71kcal	Fat:	2g
Carbohydrates:	11g	Protein:	2g

PROTEIN PEANUT BUTTER MUFFINS

BODY BUILDING

Ingredients

- 2 bananas
- 2 scoops whey protein powder
- 6 tbsp smooth peanut butter
- 2 tsp coconut oil
- 2 tbsp ground almonds

- 2 large free-range eggs
- 2 tsp coconut flour
- ½ tsp baking powder
- 1½ tsp cinnamon powder

Method

1 Preheat the oven to 350F/170C/Gas4

2 Peel and mash the bananas with the back of a fork.

3 Combine all the ingredients together to make a smooth batter.

4 Divide the batter in the six muffin cases and bake in the oven for approx. 20 minutes or until muffins have cooked through.

NUTRITION PER SERVING

Calories:	229kcal	Fat:	14g
Carbohydrates:	17g	Protein:	13g

CARROT & RAISIN MUFFINS

BODY BUILDING

Ingredients

- 1 medium carrot
- 2 scoops whey protein powder
- 50g/2oz raisins
- 50g/2oz ground almonds

- 25g/1oz ricotta cheese
- 1 tsp ground cinnamon
- ½ tsp baking powder
- 2 large free-range eggs

Method

1 Preheat the oven to 350F/170C/Gas4

2 Peel and grate the carrot.

3 Combine all the ingredients together to make a smooth batter.

4 Divide the batter in the six muffin cases and bake in the oven for approx. 20 minutes or until muffins have cooked through.

NUTRITION PER SERVING

Calories:	156kcal	Fat:	8g
Carbohydrates:	13g	Protein:	11g

PEANUT BUTTER & JELLY

BODY BUILDING

Ingredients

- 3 tbsp cottage cheese
- 2 tbsp smooth peanut butter
- 1 tbsp strawberry jam

Method

1 Place the cottage cheese in the bottom of a small bowl.

2 Dollop the peanut butter on one side and the jam on the other.

3 Serve immediately as a simple, sweet post-workout pudding

NUTRITION PER SERVING

Calories:	310kcal	Fat:	19g
Carbohydrates:	24g	Protein:	15g

CHOCOLATE 'CHEESE' MOUSSE

BODY BUILDING

Ingredients

- 200g/7oz cottage cheese
- 1 tbsp honey
- 1 tbsp unsweetened cocoa powder
- 1 tsp coconut oil
- 1 tbsp dark chocolate chips

Method

1 Use a blender to combine the cottage cheese, honey and cocoa powder into a smooth mousse.

2 Gently stir in the coconut oil and chocolate chips. Place in a small bowl and refrigerate for at least 30 minutes before serving.

NUTRITION PER SERVING

Calories:	400kcal	Fat:	20g
Carbohydrates:	37g	Protein:	24g

ALL DAY GRANOLA SWEET BOWL

BODY BUILDING

Ingredients

- 50g/2oz granola
- 2 tbsp Greek yoghurt
- 1 banana
- 25g/1oz raspberries
- 1 tbsp peanut butter
- 1 tsp honey

Method

1 Peel and slice the banana.

2 Give the raspberries a rinse under cold water and gently pat dry.

3 Arrange the granola and yoghurt in the base of a breakfast bowl and add the sliced banana and raspberries.

4 Dollop the peanut butter on top and serve with the honey drizzled over.

NUTRITION PER SERVING

Calories:	497kcal	Fat:	20g
Carbohydrates:	72g	Protein:	12g

PROTEIN BERRY 'ICE CREAM'

BODY BUILDING

Ingredients

- 2 bananas
- 300g/11oz frozen mixed berries
- 1 tbsp almond milk

- 2 scoops vanilla protein powder
- 2 tsp vanilla extract
- 2 tbsp almond butter

Method

1 Peel & slice the bananas and place in the freezer overnight.

2 When the bananas are frozen add these along with all the ingredients to a food processor and pulse until you have a lovely fruity ice cream.

3 Divide into two and freeze whatever you aren't using right away.

NUTRITION PER SERVING

Calories:	356kcal	Fat:	10g
Carbohydrates:	46g	Protein:	25g